# WHY [illegible]

# THE CHR[illegible]AN FAITH



*An address given at a Christian Watch Meeting held on 13th May 2009 in the House of Lords and hosted by Lord MacKay of Clashfern.*

BY

R. F. GRAHAM

BSc (Soc) LLB MA MBA

THE COVENANT PUBLISHING CO. LTD.

121, Low Etherley, Bishop Auckland, Co. Durham, DL14 0HA

2011

ISBN 978-085205-084-2

Printed by
THE COVENANT PUBLISHING COMPANY LIMITED
121, Low Etherley, Bishop Auckland,
Co. Durham, DL14 0HA
www.covpub.co.uk

# WHY PARLIAMENT NEEDS THE CHRISTIAN FAITH

By
R. F. Graham
BSc(Soc) LLB MA MBA

## I INTRODUCTION

## II WHY PARLIAMENT?

## III THE BROKEN STATE OF BRITISH SOCIETY TODAY

## IV WHY THE CHISTIAN FAITH-IN-PARTICULAR?

## V WHAT CRITICAL OBJECTIONS WILL BE RAISED AGAINST SUCH A CLAIM?

## VI WHAT WILL BE THE PRICE OF FAILURE?

## VII CONCLUSION

# I INTRODUCTION

I intend (in the time available to me this evening) to provide answers to the questions that follow unavoidably from the claim made in tonight's address – namely -

**WHY PARLIAMENT NEEDS THE CHRISTIAN FAITH**

Questions such as –

- **Why Parliament?**
- **Why the Christian Faith-in-Particular?**
- **What Critical Objections will be Raised against such a Claim?**
- **And What will be the Price of Failure?**

## II WHY PARLIAMENT?

**So why <u>does</u> Parliament need the Christian Faith**?

Because Parliament (or rather the Queen in Parliament) is at the very centre of our national life - and because it is Parliament that determines the very structure and functioning of civil society in terms of -

- How our nation is governed
- The content of its law
- And how justice is administered

And whatever belief system; political ideology; or religious vision that controls these three political institutions - these will determine the very moral, social and economic environment within which we as individuals, families and communities live.

If such Governmental institutions are controlled by values which are contrary to the truth of Christian revelation – then inevitably –

- Not only will we as citizens be constrained (and often forced) to act contrary to what we believe the Word of God clearly teaches
- But the whole nation will experience cultural fragmentation, institutional breakdown and increasing national decline.

## III THE BROKEN STATE OF BRITISH SOCIETY TODAY

But before I answer the remaining questions - let me comment very briefly on what is being increasingly referred to as **"the broken state of British society today."**

The problems facing our nation today are many and various – but one of the greatest difficulties we face is that a great many of our fellow citizens don't recognise that the nation is now already in great moral and physical danger.

And this is because there is an absence of a trustworthy and reliable framework that would enable them to identify what is (in fact) good and evil in the first place.

This is what the Christian Scriptures mean when it says that:

> "*My people are destroyed for lack of knowledge.*" (Hosea 4: 6)

I cannot (because of the limited time this evening) discuss in detail those many dangers – so let me select one major threat – and I do so because it is an example of a threat which poses particular danger to the most fundamental of all human institutions – the health of which is vital to the very survival of the nation – namely: the *FAMILY.*

Indeed, the traditional Christian role of parents as their children's real guardians is now greatly undermined – and the resulting breakdown and fragmentation of family structure and values has now become a reality which threatens the very stability of contemporary society.

The main moral dangers facing the family are:

- Sexual Promiscuity
- Adultery
- Sexual Perversion
- Homosexuality
- An Increasing Confusion Among the Legal, Sexual and Biological Identities of Parents and Children

- Gambling
- Alcoholism
- An Increasing Burden of Financial Debt
- And the Tyranny of a State-Imposed Immorality

Briefly then –

1. Sexual Promiscuity; Adultery; Sexual Perversion; and Homosexuality; are totally unacceptable to both the Old and New Testaments of Holy Scripture – and any one who declares otherwise is not only ignorant of God's Holy Law but is also gravely dishonest – and in rebellion against a Holy God.

The Ten Commandments and their explication in the Case Law of the Bible – are not some ancient and now-outdated system of morality – rather they are nothing less than the universal standards for human behaviour laid down by the God and Father of our Lord Jesus Christ – to whom all of humanity are held responsible – both in this life and in the life to come.

Disobedience to these God-given standards is what the Bible calls "Sin" – and consequently, their violation or abandonment will inevitably lead to judgement and (ultimately) to the very destruction of society itself.

2. Further - since it is clear from Biblical principles and the cumulative evidence of sociological research that children do best in two-parented married families with heterosexual couples as the married parents – the practice of homosexual parenthood and socially engineered alternative "family" structures seriously endanger the physical and psychological health of the children involved.

As a recent article (April 2009) from the Centre for Policy Studies titled "*We can't let the family die*" expresses it thus –

> "*...children in single and co-habiting families are more likely to*
>
> - *Suffer physical abuse*
> - *Fail at school*
> - *Play truant*
> - *Suffer from depression and other mental illnesses*
> - *Or turn to drugs and alcohol*

*The rising level of social dysfunction mirrors a rising level of family fragmentation...If the family fails, society breaks up – and there are many signs that this is happening.*"

3. Gambling; Alcoholism; and an Increasing Burden of Financial Debt are also deadly to the Family Unit and (therefore) fatal to the moral, physical and spiritual health of the nation.

4. Therefore – any Government, Legislature or Judiciary which directly or indirectly supports such destructive behaviours is (in effect) doing what the Scriptures roundly condemn – namely:

"*Woe to them that call evil good, and good evil; that put darkness for light and light for darkness;...Therefore as the fire devours the stubble, and the flame consumes the chaff, so their root shall be rottenness, and their blossom shall go up as dust: because they have cast away the law of the LORD of hosts, and despised the word of the Holy One of Israel.*" (Isaiah 5: 20-24)

And the result is that we now have an increasing Imposition of non-Christian and State-Imposed Immorality.

And please note that this area of the Family is not just a moral issue – it is also a highly political issue – and that is why it has become a central concern to Christians who are becoming increasingly disturbed (some may even say "angry") about the failure of the main political parties to recognise (never mind their failure to repair) the damage being done to our society by its departure from the tried and tested values of our Christian Heritage.

## IV WHY THE CHRISTIAN FAITH-IN-PARTICULAR?

**But why is the Christian Faith-In-Particular necessary to Parliament – or is the Christian Faith (or for that matter any other belief system or political ideology) merely optional extras to the political process?**

1. First and foremost – Parliament needs the Christian Faith because it is true – what Art Lindsley has recently called "*True Truth*".

And in John's Gospel Jesus says –

> "*...ye shall know the truth, and the truth shall make you free.*"
> (John 8: 32)

The Christian Faith is a revelation given to us by God about Himself and us.

- It explains why our world is as it is
- It tells us how it started
- How it will end
- And how we are to live in it

And the resurrection of Jesus Christ is one of the great evidences that the Gospel is true – neither the Jewish leaders nor the Romans were able to produce His body – because he had risen from the dead. Nor is there any other religion, political ideology or belief system able to offer such hope for the reformation and betterment of individuals and society!

2. But whatever you may (or may not) think of the truth claims of the Christian Faith – it has provided the moral basis of our British culture and its laws.

Since at least from the days of King Alfred the Great - British rulers have been concerned that the Bible should be at the heart of the British Constitution.

Alfred himself based his 9th Century Codification of English Law on the Ten Commandments and on legal and moral precepts from both the Old and New

Testaments – and his jurisprudence incorporated such fundamental principles as the equality of all before the law and a system of punishments that was more rational and proportionate because it was Biblical.

3. Indeed – the whole course of British history has been shaped by a continuing attempt to apply the Christian Faith to public life. And this was never truer than at the Reformation when there was a great return to the purity of the Biblical faith and a repudiation of the errors of the Church of Rome.

Other belief systems have not delivered the freedom, stability and prosperity that the Christian Faith has given the United Kingdom. **Even** the atheist and journalist Simon Heffer has (in a recent article [April 2009] in the Daily Telegraph) pointed out that the 16th Century Reformation brought with it the necessary conditions that laid the foundation for Britain's future economic development and national greatness.

4. Of course - no society in this fallen world is perfect but Christian Britain was a country where there was much that was admirable. The influence of Christian morality ennobled and elevated British society in every respect - and the Christian standards of probity, courage, integrity and faithfulness were upheld. Indeed – the British people were admired and respected throughout the world.

But now (in our own day) – we see a society in serious decline – both morally and materially. And this in turn is primarily the result of a personal and national departure from God's pure standards of equity and justice.

5. There are now (for example) many voices calling for the abolition of the Act of Settlement and the creation of a so-called secular Constitution. But it is clear that both individuals and nations need a faith-by-which-to-live.

Our Protestant Constitution has delivered great freedom and prosperity and we should not readily abandon it.

- Roman Catholicism has not produced the freedoms nor the prosperity enjoyed by Protestant countries

- Islam in its unbridled forms is a cruel enemy of political and religious liberty

- And Atheistic Communism has been responsible for some of the most repressive and murderous regimes that the world has ever seen.

It is worth remembering that during the political turmoil of the early twentieth century – our Protestant Constitutional Monarchy protected us

- not only from the follies and brutalities of the Communist Revolution
- but also from the murderous and genocidal tyranny of Fascism.

Biblical Christianity is at the heart (indeed it **is** the heart) of our British Constitution - and the evidence of history tells us that it is worth preserving.

## V WHAT CRITICAL OBJECTIONS WILL BE RAISED AGAINST SUCH A CLAIM?

**<u>But</u> what critical objections will be raised against such a claim?**

There are <u>three</u> (3) major objections which are put forward against the proposition that -

> **"Parliament needs the Christian Faith."**

1. The <u>first</u> concerns the view that <u>religion</u> must be kept out of politics because of its fundamental nature and possible disruptive effects.
2. The <u>second</u> objection is that since <u>legal supremacy</u> in the United Kingdom belongs only to the Queen in Parliament – there can be no other source of law superior to it except where Parliament allows it.
3. The <u>third</u> objection is the assertion that <u>sovereignty</u> in the United Kingdom is located in the people (i.e. in the citizens) of the United Kingdom.

1. Now the way to defeat this <u>first</u> objection (<u>namely</u> – the argument that **<u>religion</u>** must be kept out of politics) is to expose the <u>basic **mis**conception underlying it</u>. <u>Once</u> this becomes clear, the objection is (in effect) **"turned on its head"** –

And this is because - <u>politics</u> is (in fact) <u>unavoidably</u> and <u>incorrigibly</u> **"religious"**!

<u>And this is because</u> politics deal with the <u>fundamental</u> issues of our life together as <u>social</u> beings. For example – <u>politics</u> is:-

- About the rules under which we live
- About justice
- About punishment and reward
- About who gets what and why

- About war and peace
- About the nature and limits of the State
- And so on

And <u>**all**</u> of these matters are <u>religious</u> matters - <u>because</u> the political decisions that we (and others) make about these issues reflect the <u>very beliefs</u> we hold - <u>beliefs</u>

- about what is right and wrong
- about whether there is a right and wrong in the first place
- about who and what we are
- about to whom we are ultimately responsible
- And so on

<u>And</u> - <u>such beliefs</u> (in turn) are ultimately <u>matters of faith</u> – in other words – they are about what is meant when we use the concept **"religion"**

<u>And therefore</u> - secular-humanism, socialism, conservatism, and nationalism are <u>just as much</u> **faith-based belief-systems** as are Christianity, Islam, Buddhism, etc.

<u>In other words</u> – the argument that <u>**religion**</u> must be kept out of politics is often nothing more than <u>self-serving nonsense</u> - put out by those <u>secular</u> politicians who are desperate to <u>exclude</u> significant challenges to their <u>equally</u> "religious" viewpoints – <u>Indeed</u> such objections are <u>not only</u> nonsense - they are -

***"Nonsense-on-Stilts!"***

2. However – the <u>second</u> objection is not totally mistaken.

   1. <u>At one level</u> – the doctrine of the **legal supremacy** of the Queen in Parliament is perfectly acceptable as a <u>formal</u> rule of the British Constitution - to the effect that there are <u>no</u> legitimate executive, legislative and judicial powers <u>apart from</u> those exercised by the authority of the Queen in Parliament.

   2. <u>But</u> to use a <u>formal</u> rule of the British Constitution to support an argument to the effect that the **Christian** <u>value-system</u> cannot be allowed to form the <u>content</u> of our legislation - on the grounds that it is (in some pejorative sense) a "religion" – **<u>or</u>** (**<u>alternatively</u>**) that a **Christian** value-system somehow violates the <u>legal</u> <u>supremacy</u> of the Queen in Parliament - is completely irrational - <u>or</u> to put it more bluntly – it is just plain daft!

**And why is this so?** – <u>Because</u> the <u>content</u> of <u>every</u> legal system <u>inevitably reflects</u> the predominant Value-System of that culture.

There are (in fact) <u>no</u> such things as value-free political decisions – it is **<u>only</u>** really a question of **<u>whose</u> values** should determine the **<u>actual</u> content** of governmental, legislative and judicial decisions.

It is (therefore) <u>never</u> a choice between religion and no religion – <u>rather</u> it is always <u>and</u> only a question of **<u>which</u> Religion** rules supreme in the Public arena.

And it is (**therefore**) –

- **<u>either</u>** the values of the Christian faith that will determine the policies of our Government <u>and</u> the content of our law

- **<u>or</u>** it will be some <u>other</u> belief system (<u>such as</u> secular-humanism, socialism, <u>or</u> some other political ideology) that will determine the future of our society.

**Which brings us back to the choice God gives to His people in every generation** -

- <u>Either</u> "*life and good...and blessing*"

- <u>Or</u> "*death and evil...and cursing*" (Deuteronomy 30: 15, 19)

Consequently - the Holy Scriptures solemnly warn the leaders of our nation that -

"*There is a way which seemeth right unto a man, but the end thereof are the ways of death.*" (Proverbs 14:12 & 16:25)

Indeed – our secular political parties are leading our society into a moral wilderness whose end result will be the destruction of life itself – for so does a Holy God rebuke the nations saying that:

"*...all they that hate me love death.*" (Proverbs 8: 36)

3. The third objection is not only related to the first two objections but it is also much more fundamental since it deals with the location of **sovereignty** in our society –

- i.e. who or what possesses supreme and independent authority? – or (put otherwise) who or what should determine the content of law?

Now without going into too much of a technical discussion – let me briefly make a number of points – especially in relation to our own political system here in the United Kingdom.

There are those who would argue that sovereignty (in the sense of who or what should determine the content of law) lies in the State itself - and that (therefore) sovereignty is exercised by those who control (for the time being) the law-making power of the State.

**And** a specifically modern aspect of this approach is that while the making and implementation of law is the function of the State – the actual determination of the content of the law lies in **the people** (i.e. in **the voters**). And this is often referred to as "political" sovereignty as distinguished from "legal" supremacy - **and** it is exercised through the processes of representative democracy whereby **political party policies** are translated into law and implemented by those who control (for the time being) the institutions of the State.

HOWEVER – there are many who would not wish to leave it there – **because** such an approach would make the very content of the law both arbitrary and relative.

CONSEQUENTLY – there are some who argue that there are (indeed – that there must be) at least some values which do not alter; which are not relative; and which are not arbitrary.

- That (for example) **ideas of right and wrong**; **institutions such as the family**; and certain political values such as **individual freedom** and **the separation of powers** - **cannot** simply be a matter of subjective preference. In other words - that there **is** (and there **must** be) some absolute standard of value against which all human legislation must be measured as to its justice or equity. This alternative view has a much longer history - and it is generally referred to as "**natural law**."

It is (however) vital to note that there are (what I would call) "weak" and "strong" versions of this natural law approach.

- The **weaker** version holds that any such absolute standards that exist must be based on (and subject to) the process of human reason

- But the second (and **stronger Christian**) version asserts that the God and Father of our Lord Jesus Christ has authoritatively revealed His absolute standards of equity and justice in Holy Scripture - and **this is** where we Christians **must** stand!

NOW - it is also most important to note that not so very long ago in our own nation, the concept of **sovereignty** was **not** (in fact) applied to human government. Instead – it was generally recognised that **only God** possessed supreme and independent authority and jurisdiction! In other words – **only God** (and **God alone**) should (**and already has** in Holy Scripture) revealed the content of human law.

- **Thus** - while He delegates authority to human governments (hence Romans 13: "*...the powers that be are ordained of God.*") – they (nevertheless) remain accountable to Him as the Supreme Lawgiver.

- And (further) that all human governments are being judged for any violation of His Law. Indeed – this is the very essence of **sin** – "*...for sin is the transgression of the law*" (1 John 3: 4) – and that law is the law of God!

- But – it is even worse – because human governments create by legislation the legal framework within which we live – and if that legal framework allows or enforces **in**justice; **ini**quity; **im**morality; **un**righteousness – then such human governments will become subject to the overwhelming anger of a holy and just God.

It is (therefore) essential to the achievement of true justice that human law be congruent to the law of God as given in Holy Scripture.

And therefore all human systems practise (or fail to practise) justice — to the extent that they implement (or fail to implement) **God's** law.

There is (therefore) **only one sovereignty** – and it belongs to **God alone**. And for human governments to claim an independent or separate right to determine the content of law is nothing less than rebellion – and is (in effect) national suicide!

**And indeed** – our Queen's Oath of Coronation clearly states the **Christian Biblical** basis of the Constitution of the United Kingdom **and** its devolved institutions - **and** it also clearly indicates the **Christian** and **Covenantal** status of the United Kingdom for all the world to see.

The point at issue here is that (in terms of our nation) - the God and Father of our Lord Jesus Christ is our **only Sovereign** - and is (therefore) the **only** legitimate source of our law!

Therefore – the third objection fails!

## VI WHAT WILL BE THE PRICE OF FAILURE?

**<u>But</u> what will be (and indeed – already is) the <u>price of failure</u> – i.e. <u>our</u> failure to uphold and strengthen the Christian Vision at this time in our nation's history?**

A <u>Christian</u> approach to politics <u>must</u> depend on a much deeper understanding of the nature of man <u>and</u> of the destiny of nations. <u>And</u> this in turn rests upon what we believe to be the very truth about God: His revelation of Himself as God the Father; and as God the Son; and as God the Holy Spirit - <u>Who together as One God</u> decided to save His People from their sins by the life, death, resurrection and return of our Lord Jesus Christ.

<u>This</u> (of course) is <u>nothing less than</u> a summary of the core message of the Bible - <u>and</u> the Bible itself is <u>nothing less than</u> the very Word of God <u>inscripturated</u> (i.e. our Lord Jesus Christ communicated to us in written revelation).

The Bible is **<u>also</u>** the disclosure of the nature, purpose and works of God in human history <u>and</u> contains the law of God for <u>all</u> of mankind – for individuals, for families, communities, nations and groups of nations.

In terms of what I am talking about this evening - this means (<u>and</u> Scripture clearly teaches) that <u>human government</u> is an ordinance of God for the benefit of mankind. And to the extent to which the nations <u>obey</u> the law of God as contained in the Bible – to that extent (<u>and</u> to that extent <u>only</u>) are they blessed.

**Thus** - our British Constitution clearly demonstrates the imprint of Biblical Christianity; **and** the Coronations of our Kings and Queens manifestly display <u>the centrality of the</u> <u>Christian Faith</u> to the legal, political and social history of the peoples of these British Isles.

**<u>For</u>** the nations of England, Scotland, Wales and Ireland have a precious <u>heritage</u> of Christian faith dating back to the very first century of the Christian era - **and** Britain <u>also</u> experienced that great revival of "*the faith which was once delivered to the saints*" which we know in our history as **the Protestant Reformation**.

- And as a result – our British culture and institutions reflect two thousand years of Christian faith and practice.

- And this (in turn) has produced those great legal and political principles of the **Rule of Law; Freedom Under the Law; the Separation of Powers; Democratic Accountability; and a Constitutional Monarchy** - all of which have become the central characteristics of our British Constitution.

**However** - the **un**avoidable consequence of a nation's disobedience to God's law is also true – and to the extent that governments **fail** to govern their people according to the law of God, **then** those nations are in rebellion against a Holy God - **and** they become the objects of His judgement.

And these principles apply to Christian and non-Christian nations alike.

**But** those nations (such as our own) who have known the Christian Gospel are all the more blameworthy if they fail to proclaim **and** demonstrate the Gospel of the Kingdom of our Lord Jesus Christ to a world lost in sin – and it is therefore the **Christian** nations who all the more **deserve** the judgement of a Holy God.

**Indeed** – in a very real sense – the British nation is already experiencing God's judgement as is evidenced by

- the rapid break-down of our once Christian culture and values

- the increase of individual and social evil

- and a progressive loss of our national identity as a Christian nation.

The **solution** (therefore) to our own particular situation of a nation-under-judgement - is a new Reformation and a return to Biblical Christianity.

**Thus** - the true Constitution of a Christian nation must be the very Word of God itself – as given by the law of God summarised in the Ten Commandments and explicated in the jurisprudence of the Bible.

For **true Sovereignty** (i.e. the final and supreme authority over all of life) is **not** located in The People; **nor** in The Queen in Parliament; **nor** in any other human institution or man-made ideology – **but** can be found **only** in the God and Father of our Lord Jesus Christ. For Christ alone is "*...the way, the truth, and the life*:"

**Indeed** - this is the primordial (i.e. the original) **model** of the Godly Nation given to us in Holy Scripture when we are told in Genesis 26 that God would bless **Isaac** and that through **Isaac** all the nations of the earth would be blessed because (as God said) -

> ***"...Abraham obeyed my voice, and kept my charge, my commandments, my statutes, and my laws."*** (Genesis 26: 5)

That this is no new or novel approach to political authority in Britain can be seen from our Christian forefathers.

For example - it was **John Wyclif**, the Morning Star of the Reformation, who wrote in his General Prologue to the Wyclif Bible of 1384 that "*This Bible is for the government of the people, by the people and for the people*" – well pre-dating Abraham Lincoln's Gettysburg Address of 1865.

Both **Martin Luther** and **John Calvin** distinguished the 3-fold use of **the Moral Law** as follows:

1. First – the law of God to supply the legal foundation for civil society – the *usus politicus* – this is the governmental (i.e. the political) use of the law of God
2. Second – the law of God to convict mankind of sin and of their need for a Saviour - the *usus pedagogocus* – the law as a schoolmaster to lead us to Christ
3. Third – the law of God to provide the standard of Godly behaviour – *the usus normativus* – the law to teach us what (in practice) it means to love God and to love our neighbour

And it was the Scottish theologian **Samuel Rutherford** who argued in his *Lex Rex (of 1644)* that the Law of God is King – over both Church and State: an explicit refutation of the doctrine that the content of law is from the King or governmental power or human reason.

**Therefore** – the more balanced (and certainly the more Biblically correct viewpoint) is the product of the Protestant Reformation and of the experience of both England and Scotland during the 17th Century - namely: that the Church and State are separate yet co-ordinate institutions that exist for the benefit of civil society, and both of which derive their authority from the God and Father of our Lord Jesus Christ - as revealed in the Law of God contained in the Bible. Hence the Word of God is Sovereign over both Church and State - and, indeed, over all of civil society.

Therefore – the executive, the legislative, and the judicial powers of our British nation must be subject to God and His law as contained in Holy Scripture.

For – as Scripture warns us –

> "*Righteousness exalteth a nation: but sin is a reproach to any people.*" (Proverbs 14: 34)

And again that –

> "*Where there is no vision, the people perish: but he that keepeth the law, happy is he.*" (Proverbs 29: 18)

And finally –

> "*Except the LORD build the house, they labour in vain that build it: except the LORD keep the city, the watchman waketh but in vain.*" (Psalm 127: 1)

## VII CONCLUSION

**In Conclusion – let me make two final comments.**

1. As civil society increasingly disintegrates and as explicitly non-Christian value systems proliferate and gain control of our leading institutions, the need for a resurgence of our historic Christian Faith becomes essential - if our nation is not to end up in the dustbin of history.

And because Parliament (or rather the Queen in Parliament) is (or should be) the governing power of our nation – then it is through Parliament that such a fundamental return to Christian values must come.

In particular –

- The family and the unborn child must be protected by our legislators
- We need a social and economic framework that will encourage the hard work and honesty that are the only sure foundations for a prosperous and healthy nation
- We need a legal system that punishes crime appropriately and proportionately and acts as a real deterrent
- And we need to recognise the limits of the State's authority in monitoring the lives of its citizens

2. But finally – while Parliament and the nation need the Christian faith – so do individuals!

The Apostle John said that

> "*God so loved the world that he gave his only begotten Son, that whosoever believeth in him should not perish, but have everlasting life.*"

The Christian Gospel is the Good News of the promise of eternal life to all who will put their trust in Jesus Christ.

The Christian Faith (therefore) can -

- not only heal our broken society

- but it also offers present forgiveness and eternal assurance to our fellow citizens

- **And** it provides the basis for the recovery that we desperately need at this time in our nation's history.

Thank You.

---

RFG – 13/5/2009

Underlining and **Bold** for the purpose of lecture delivery.

Brief biographical note:

**Robert** [Bob] **Fleming Graham**
BSc(Soc) LLB [London] MA [Essex] MBA [Strathclyde]

Bob Graham by sovereign grace committed his life to Christ at the age of fifteen.

After leaving school early at sixteen and working in various minor employments, he joined HM land forces, was commissioned as an infantry officer, served with the King's African Rifles and later, briefly, with the RAOC, before taking voluntary retirement to join HM Foreign Office as a junior official.

In his early thirties he left HM Foreign and Commonwealth Office to begin university level study and now has degrees in sociology, law, politics, and business administration from the Universities of London, Essex and Strathclyde.

Over the last four decades he has been a college lecturer, university administrator, Conservative Parliamentary Candidate (1983 and 1987 General Elections) and Deputy Director and Company Secretary of a private educational and training institute serving the international maritime industry.

He is married to Heather, has two sons and two daughters and is a Member of St George's-Tron Church of Scotland, Glasgow.

Now retired, he maintains a close interest in contemporary politics, and is now a Member of (and has been a Candidate in the Scottish Parliamentary Elections of 2007 for) the Christian Party: Proclaiming Christ's Lordship.